When you wish upon a star

makes no difference who you are.

Anything your heart desires will come to you.

If your heart is in your dreams

no request is too extreme.

When you wish upon a star as dreamers do . . .

"When You Wish Upon a Star"

lyrics by Ned Washington

Ballerina Dreams

a true story

by Lauren Thompson

Photographs by James Estrin

FEIWEL AND FRIENDS

New York

NICOLE

SHEKINAH

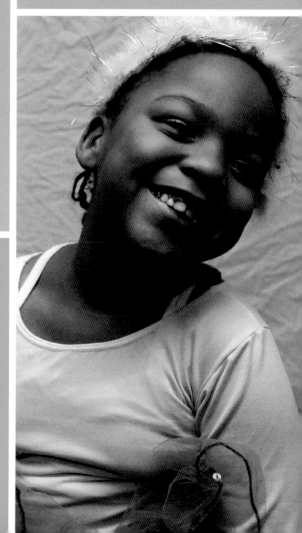

VERONICA

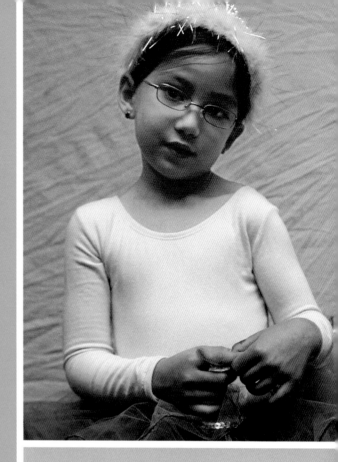

ABBEY

MONICA

ONCE UPON A TIME, there were five little girls who had a dream. They dreamed of being ballerinas. They wanted to wear tutus and tiaras and dance onstage for the whole world to see. They wanted to dance just like other little girls.

The girls had a dream, but they knew it wouldn't be easy to make this dream come true. They had cerebral palsy or other muscle disorders, and their muscles wouldn't move exactly the way they wanted them to. Some had trouble raising their arms, or holding themselves upright. Some found it hard to keep their balance. Some used wheelchairs or walkers to get around.

The girls knew that fulfilling their dream would take a lot of hard work. But they were ready to work hard. They knew that they might never move in the same way that other ballerinas move. But they were eager to find out what they could do. All they wanted was the chance to be the best ballerinas they could be.

Once, there were five little girls who dreamed of being ballerinas. And they made their dream come true.

Ballet class is about to start, and the girls are hurrying to get ready. They pull off their coats and shoes, and pull on their ballet slippers and tutus. They look forward to class all week long. They love dancing to the elegant music, and they love their teacher, Joann.

Joann loves this class, too. She hands out silver crowns and sparkling wands to all the dancers. She wants each girl — Nicole, Abbey, Monica, Shekinah, and Veronica — to feel like a ballerina princess.

Joann makes every dancer feel like a star.

The girls love wearing their leotards, tutus, and ballet slippers. Some wear leg braces to help them stand and to help their leg muscles develop properly.

Today's class is special. The girls have worked hard all year. Week after week, they have practiced positions and moves that were difficult for them until they weren't so difficult anymore. Their bodies have gotten stronger. They have learned to reach farther and stand taller than ever. Now they are ready to show the world what they can do. Tomorrow, they will dance onstage in their own ballet recital. The recital will be called "Wishes and Dreams."

First, the girls warm up at the barre. They stretch their legs out behind them and their arms out in front. They bend their knees in *plié*.

(right) Joann helps Monica get into position at the barre, while Abbey stretches. Monica has focused on improving her balance. Now she is learning to stand using her new cane.

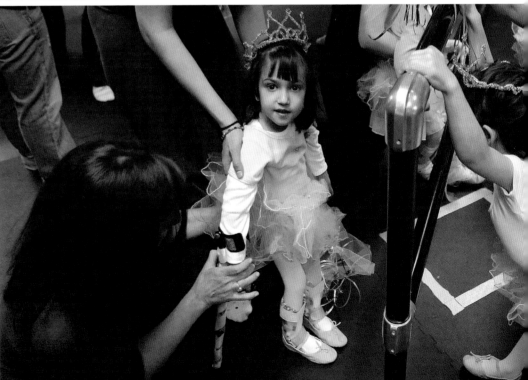

(above) The girls practice their *pliés*. They all have helpers, who are there to help them balance or hold their positions as they dance.

Then the girls move to the floor to rehearse for the recital one last time. They point one leg out front, in *point tendu*, and reach forward as far as they can. They hold their arms up high, sway from side to side, and turn. By the end of the class, the girls are squirming with excitement. The next time they dance together, they will be onstage.

As the girls get ready to leave, a few ask Joann, "What if I turn the wrong way? What if I drop my wand?"

"Just smile and keep going," she says. "That's what ballerinas do."

Joann leads the class through the dances they will perform in the recital. Each girl completes the steps to the best of her ability.

The next morning, the girls gather backstage at the recital hall. The first dance will be from *The Nutcracker*, and they are all dressed as the Sugar Plum Fairy, with flowing pink and white ribbons. The helpers brush the girls' hair smooth. They help the girls put on makeup — lots of glittery eye shadow, sparkling blusher, and shiny lipstick. The girls look in the mirror and are amazed. They look like prima ballerinas!

Backstage, the girls enjoy fussing over their costumes, hair, and makeup. There are twenty-one sparkling shades of eye shadow to choose from, and lots of glittery hairspray.

The dancers peek from behind the curtain as the audience comes in. They see their parents and families sitting in the front rows. Their friends, neighbors, classmates, and teachers are there, too.

Some of the girls are excited and giggly. Some are quiet, hoping they remember the dance steps once they are onstage. Joann gathers everyone together. She reminds them to take a deep breath, be proud, and smile their ballerina smiles.

"So, are we ready?" she asks.

The girls shout, "YES!"

It's showtime!

"So, are we ready?"
"YES!"

The dancers and their helpers take their places onstage. Then the music of *The Nutcracker* begins, and the curtains swing open as the audience cheers. The girls grin gleefully and start to dance. Soon, they're all having too much fun to be nervous.

And they dance beautifully. When the melody seems to rise and swirl, the girls raise their arms and turn, and their ribbons float in the air. Onstage, under the bright lights, they feel like real ballerinas at last.

Before the girls know it, the music ends and the first part of the recital is over. They hurry backstage to change costumes.

(above) Veronica turns as her helper steadies her. This year, Veronica has worked hard to strengthen her torso and legs so that she can hold herself up straighter.

(left) At the last minute, Nicole (far left) feels nervous about going onstage. But once the familiar music starts, she feels more at ease. And she can see her parents and baby sister smiling at her from the audience.

The next dance is from *Swan Lake*. The girls chose the dance because they love this story about a princess who never gives up. And they love the idea of wearing feathers. Lots of feathers! Now, with their helpers' assistance, they pull on white feathery tutus and white feathery crowns, and grab their white feathery fans. By the time the dancers are ready, feathers are floating everywhere.

(above) At first, Abbey had trouble moving her left arm. Every week, she pushed herself a little farther, and now she can lift it well. She loves ballet so much that she practices every day at home.

Like young Swan Queens, the ballerinas spread their wings and take flight. Many of the girls have seen their sisters, cousins, and friends perform in ballet recitals. Now, it is their turn.

Back onstage, the music from *Swan Lake* begins. The dancers bend low, like sleeping swans, and then they rise as if they are taking off in flight. They open their fans, which sweep through the air like graceful wings.

Shekinah has wanted to be onstage in a tutu since she was very young, and she can hardly contain her excitement.

Backstage again, the girls change into blue tutus and sparkling tiaras for the show's finale. Then, one last time, they take their places onstage.

The music begins to play, and the curtains are drawn open. This time, each helper holds up a shiny silver star. One by one, each girl reaches to take her star from her helper's hand and calls out her name for all to hear. *Nicole. Abbey. Monica. Shekinah. Veronica.* Their clear voices are full of pride.

A voice sings with the music: "When you wish upon a star…" The ballerinas lift their stars high above their heads and sway. They turn gracefully one last time, and then the music ends. One of the girls yells, "Yea, we did it!" And the audience cheers.

Monica, Shekinah, and Veronica hold their silver stars. Their perseverance and hard work has brought them to this joyful moment.

WISHES AND DREAMS

(above) Joann gives a red rose to each girl. Today, they are all prima ballerinas.

(left) The girls' families give them lots of love and encouragement as they dream their dreams and strive to make them come true.

Joann comes onstage to hand each girl a red rose. "I'm so proud of you all!" she says. Everyone has tears in their eyes. But they are not tears of sadness. They are tears of joy. The girls dreamed of being ballerinas, and they have made their dream come true.

Monica has planned her own special finale. Her helper will let go, and for the first time in front of her father, who is in the audience, Monica will stand using just her cane.

MEET THE

Abbey, age 4

Abbey did not have much strength in her left arm due to a condition called Erb's palsy, which was caused by nerve damage at birth. For the recital, she practiced hard to be able to bring both arms into position. She plays "ballerina" with her friends whenever she can.

Monica, age 5

Monica is small for her age, but very strong. At first, she hung back in ballet class, but now she participates eagerly. Her impaired balance has made it difficult to stand and walk on her own. But she has learned to walk with the help of a walker and stand using her cane.

Nicole, age 3

Nicole is the youngest of the group. All year, she focused on making her right side stronger and on improving her balance. By the time of the recital, she was able to turn partway around on her own. She uses a walker to get around her preschool.

BALLERINAS

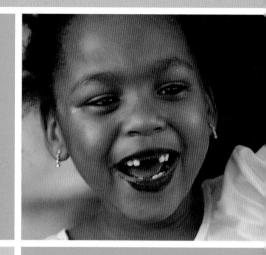

Shekinah, age 5

Shekinah loves to be onstage. When class began, she needed a lot of support to stand, but now she can briefly stand on her own. At school, she moves from class to class using a walker, and also uses her strong arms to push herself in her wheelchair.

Veronica, age 7

When Veronica started class three years ago, she had difficulty sitting by herself. Now she can sit alone, and with support, she can stand. Her arms and hands are getting stronger, too. With her motorized wheelchair, she has no trouble keeping up with her friends.

MORE ABOUT JOANN

Joann Ferrara, the girls' ballet teacher, is a physical therapist and the owner of Associated Therapies in Bayside (Queens), New York. The girls, who have cerebral palsy (or, in one case, Erb's palsy,) receive physical therapy, sometimes several times a week, and some have since infancy. Joann heard from many parents how much their girls wanted to take ballet class just like their friends did, but that regular ballet classes couldn't accommodate children with disabilities. Four years ago, Joann decided to offer her own ballet class as a supplement to physical therapy.

"It's important to focus on the children's abilities, not their disabilities," she says. "At first, the girls may have difficulty standing on their own, or even sitting up. But I encourage them to be proud of what they *can* do, and of any progress they make. Every new ability is a tremendous achievement for them."

MORE ABOUT THE HELPERS

Each girl has her own helper who assists her in class and performs with her onstage during the recital. They range in age from eleven to sixteen, and they volunteer for the program for a variety of reasons. One helper sees her beloved grandmother struggling with increasing disabilities and wants to help her and others overcome their limitations. Another has a cousin with CP. Each helper has come to know when her younger partner needs support — perhaps with sitting, or holding her arms in position — and when she is ready to try something on her own. Their dedication is extraordinary: One helper travels an hour from home to attend the weekly class. The close bond between the girls and their helpers is yet another way that the ballet program fosters pride and confidence in all the young people involved.

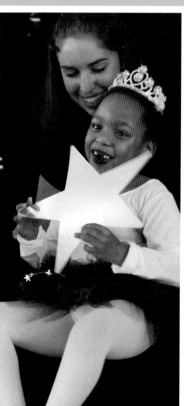

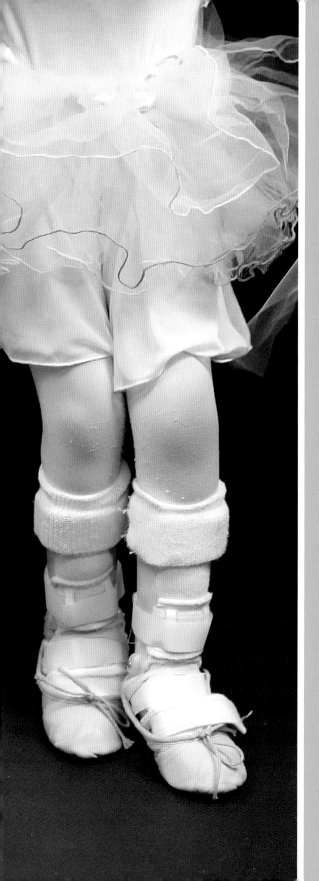

MORE ABOUT CEREBRAL PALSY

Most of the girls in Joann's ballet class have cerebral palsy [*seh-**ree**-brawl* **pawl**-zee*], or CP. This is a condition in which a person's brain and muscles aren't able to communicate well. Often, CP is the result of the brain not getting enough oxygen at the time of birth. It isn't an illness, and it doesn't "spread" from one person to another like a cold. CP also doesn't affect a person's intelligence. Joann's girls all attend regular school.

CP can cause several kinds of difficulties. Sometimes certain muscles can't easily relax, forcing a foot to point or a hand to clench. Sometimes muscles are weak, or don't move smoothly, or are hard to control. In other cases, the part of the brain that tells muscles how to keep the body in balance is affected. People with cerebral palsy may have only one difficulty in one part of the body, or a combination of difficulties in many parts of the body.

Cerebral palsy can't be cured, but with physical therapy, occupational therapy, and activities like Joann's ballet class, people with CP can train their muscles to be as strong, flexible, and responsive as possible. The work can be tiring and difficult, and the progress that can be made in each case is always unknown. But the determination shown by these young dancers will help ensure that they reach their full potential.

Meet Joann's ballet class of 2007!